Şhạdẹş of Ḷịfẹ

I0089199

Published by I Ain't Your Marionette

P.O BOX 184
Larder Lake, ON P0K 1L0
http://iaintyourmarionette.com

Layout, and design by Marie D. Moldovan
Edited by Marie D. Moldovan and Alycia Hodge.

About Shades of Life

I authored this book of poetry as a way of getting my thoughts and feelings down. I started writing poetry as a young girl; as I got older, I wrote about loss, death, love, and motherhood. I hope that the poems in this book help the reader in times of hardship and in times of happiness.

What people are saying about Shades of Life:

There is a fine line between love and hate, light and dark, good and bad, some may even say there's only a shade difference between them all. Two emotions seemingly opposite one another, but in fact they're lighter and darker shades of the same feeling.

This book, "Shades of Life" blends those emotions, exposing the hues of the human experience so honestly. Shade is a result of how light or dark a color appears to its counterparts, and that effect can be seen in our life experiences as expressed in "Shades of Life."

From the dark stains of tragedy to the bright tones of innocence and triumph, Emma Hilson-Gregory casts an array of tints and tinges across these pages in the form of colorful penmanship. Accompanying the words are shadows, coolness, and intensity in the form of black-and-white artwork and imagery that live amongst the shade cast by the author's mighty pen.

The illustrator, Marie Moldovan crosshatches the words to the artwork with a perfect understanding of light and darkness that brings playful images from the shadows and fills in the shadows with a darkness that is felt. This read spans the emotional spectrum, from tapping into the inner child to triggering the heavier-hearted realities of life.

--Joe Mykut,
Author of *Beautiful Boy*

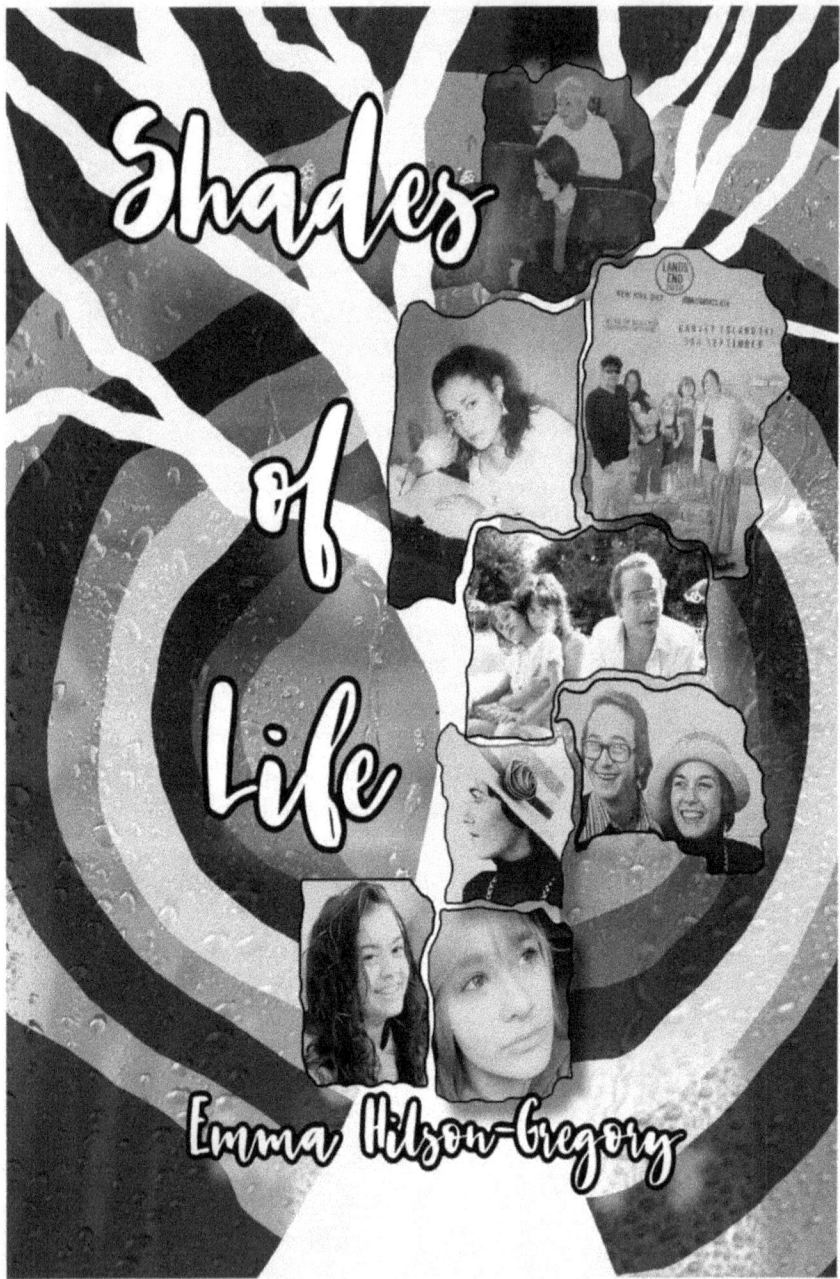

DEDICATED TO:

Amanda, Rodney, Inky, Chookie, Sheila, Tony, Riley, James, Indiannah and Dekota.
You all made me the person I am ---
whether that was growing up without you in my life or with you in my life ---
walking with me through this journey called life.
Thank you.
　　X

Foreword
By Alycia Hodge

Life is not always black and white. Life, death, past, and future are not always easily understood. Varying shades of gray cover the questionable areas where we long for simple and straightforward answers. Sometimes all we can do is accept the unknowable, embrace the joys between the hard moments, show compassion to ourselves and others, and pose our inner questions and answers in art forms, as some things can be expressed no other way.

The poems in this book reminded me of my strength as a mother, woman, and human being. It reminded me that it is ok to cry and to sometimes not feel ok. It reminded me that every big and small joy should be cherished. It reminded me that hope can always be found, even in the darkest times. It reminded me I am never alone on this rollercoaster of life, as the emotions found in these pages stretch across all boundaries.

Life does not always go how we think or expect it should, but our will to carry on and hold onto love and hope is part of the wonder of living.

Table of Contents

✳✳✳

Table of Contents
✳✳✳

Table of Contents
✳✳✳

Chapter 1:
Children's Poems

Valentine

Caroline, Caroline, will you be my Valentine?
If you will bowl and never bat~~~
Share your sweets and hold my rat~~~
And never, never whine~~~
You may be my Valentine ~~~

"Julian, Howard, Randolph, Sam"
Who on earth do you think I am?

If you want a valentine try someone else,
For I have mine. ~~~

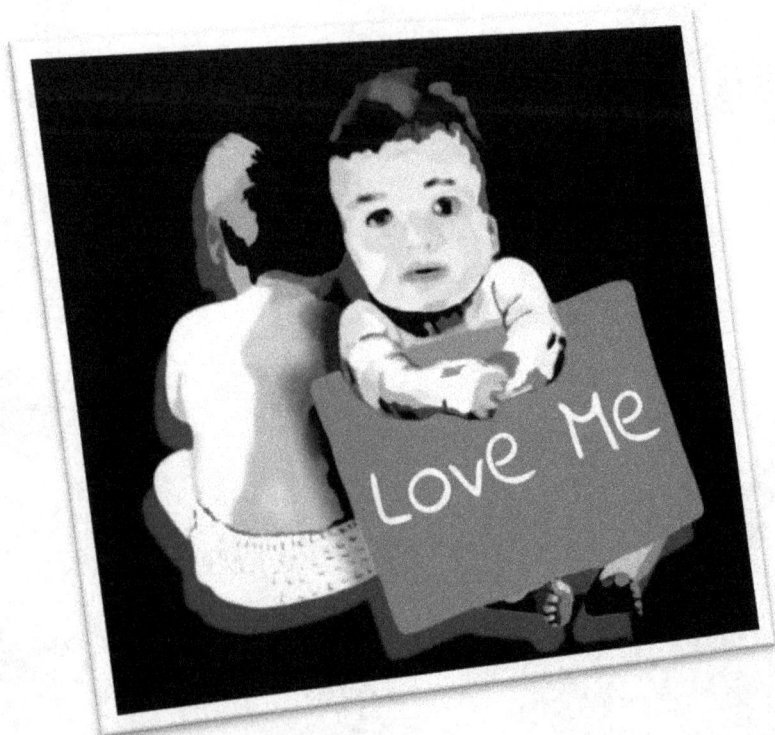

The Shadows

The shadows on the nursery wall
are strange and squat and thin and tall~~~

They change so fast, it's hard to see what on earth
they're meant to be at all. ~~~

Down with Mondays

Down with Mondays,
that's what I say.
All work no play;
worst day of the week. ~~~

Beastly-soggy-washing day,
cold meat, and beetroot day. ~~~

Down with Mondays, that's what I say. ~~~

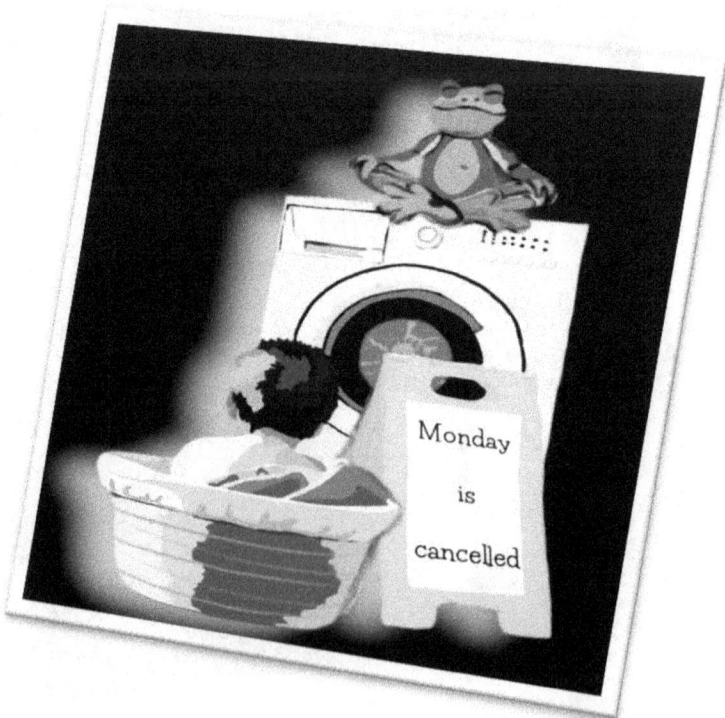

The Skynx

Did you know that the Skynx
just sits there and thinks,
lying on the branch of a tree? ~~~

He just nods, blinks, enjoys forty winks,
and looks as kind as can be. ~~~

And although he's admired
he is always tired
and he yawns when it's time for tea. ~~~

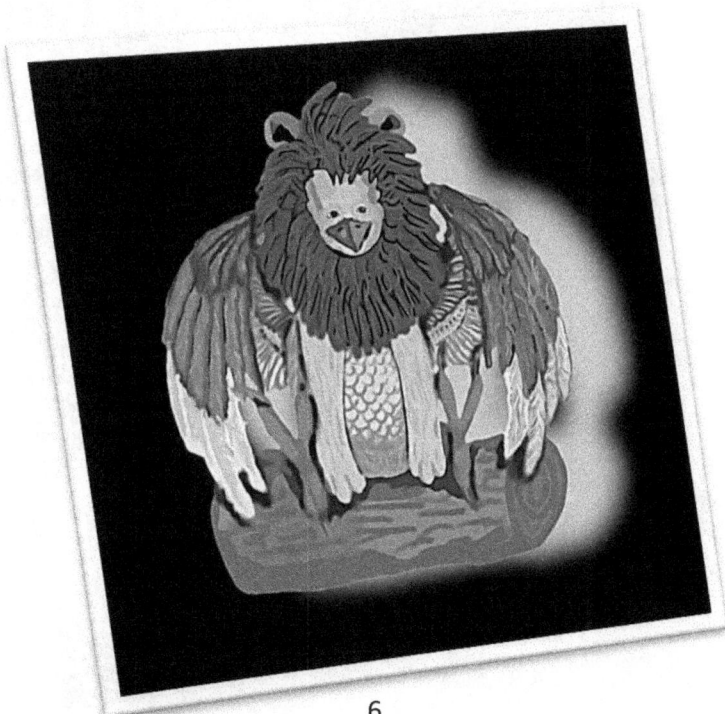

6

Riddle

riddle me,
riddle – me – ree,
a man in a tree
a stick in his hand,
a stone in his throat,
if you read me this riddle,
I'll give you a groat. ~~~

By the Sea

I'm going down for a day at the sea,
such wonderful things are waiting for me. ~~~

Tossing white horses and schooners with sails,
starfish with fingers, and mermaids with tails. ~~~

Magic sandcastles and fishes with wings,
sea monsters spouting and pirates with rings. ~~~

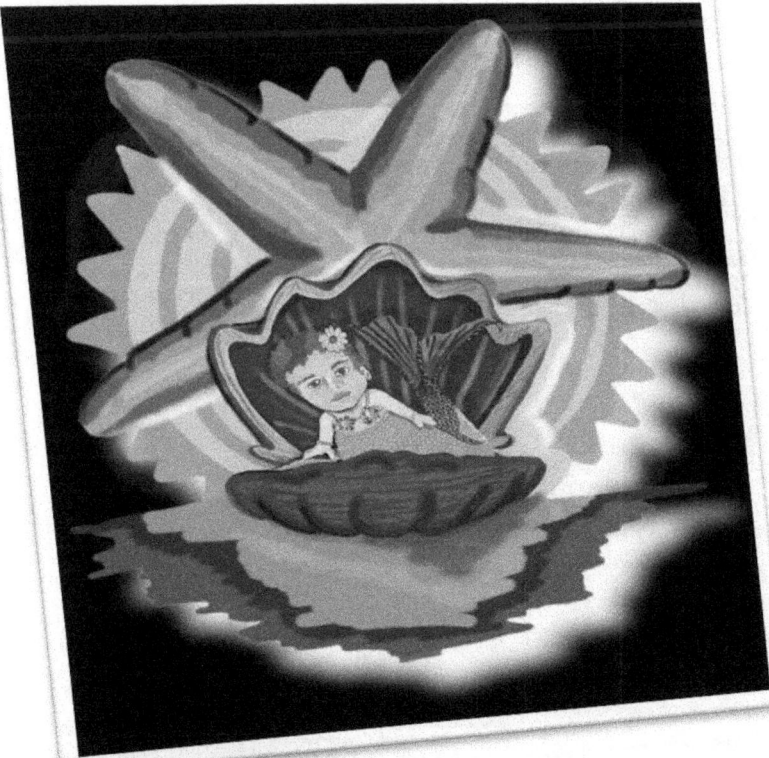

Sarah's Poem

There was a mouse living in my house. ~~~
I said, "For heaven's sake."

Your squeaky talk and tapping walk
are keeping me awake. ~~~

The mouse stopped dead and turned its head. ~~~
It said, "I beg your pardon!"

I'd rather freeze on a piece of cheese
than move into your garden. ~~~

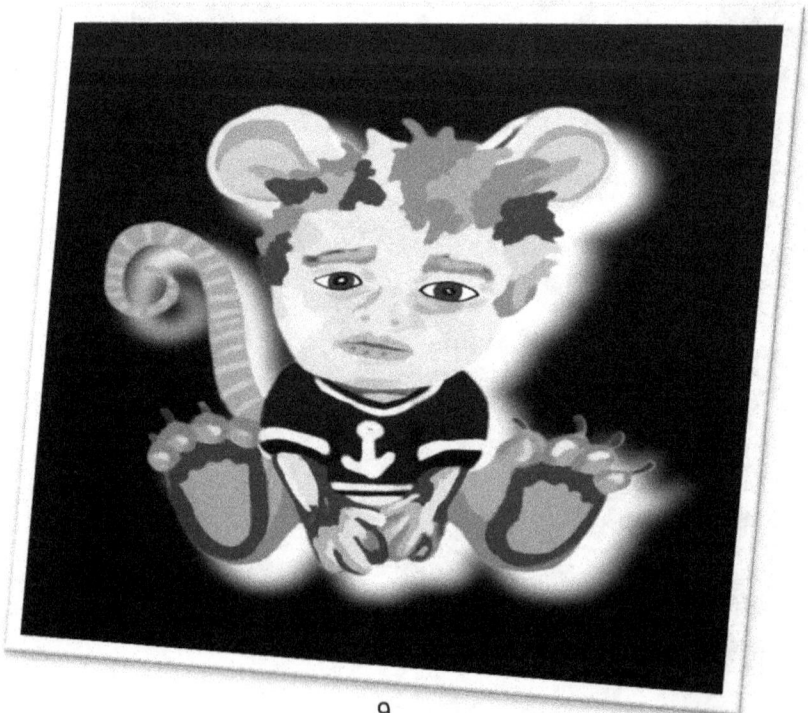

Life's Light

The light of life is so unique;
it's like the laughter of a newborn babe
the way she coos and gurgles at you~~~

Little one you seem to have a language that's yours
alone~~~

Chapter 2:
Depression

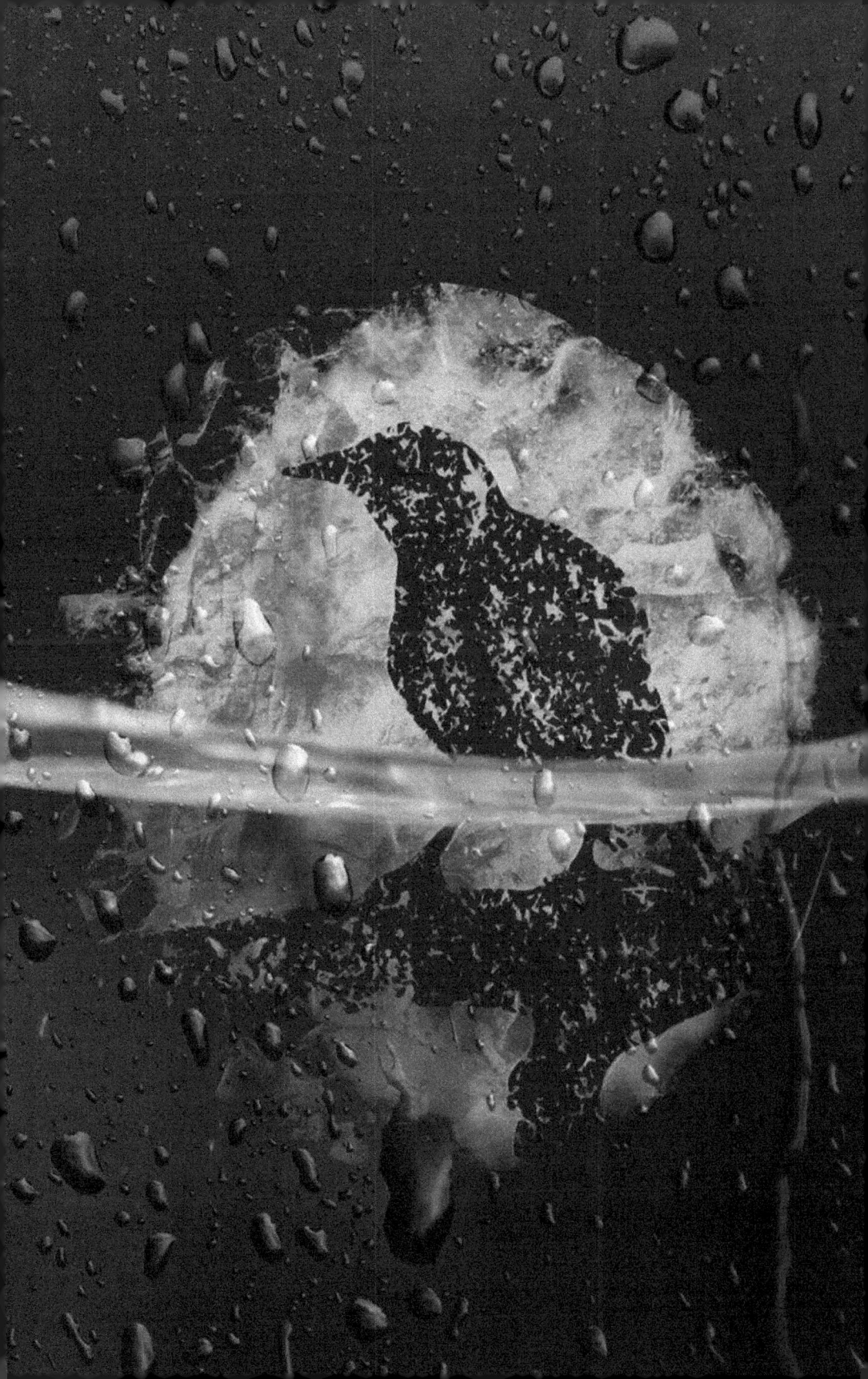

Casting Pebbles

I lie here in the darkness of my room
and cast pebbles into the dark black pools
that are in the depths of my mind. ~~~

I hear a startling noise, a rustling
of leaves, I think it seems to be,
coming from that weeping willow tree. ~~~

I look up to see a very pale boy;
he can't be more than ten. ~~~

He is not aware that I am looking in his direction
and just carries on tugging at the branches of the
tree. ~~~

He is in a solitary world of his own,
just him and the weeping willow tree. ~~~

This sad, solitary scene makes me think of
something from my childhood;
a poem that I heard I think somewhere. ~~~

"Weeping willow with your leaves hanging down,
Why do you always weep and frown?
Is it because the summer's glory must always
end in gloom and doom? ~~~

Is it because she had gone too soon?

13

Twilight

In the early hours of evening,
as day drifts towards a star-studded night;
We all discover in the twilight hours
our own secret obsessions and knowledge
for the things that seem alienated to us. ~~~

In these silent times, I feel trapped like the small
songbird who longs to be free.
Who is able to spread his wings and fly away? ~~~

At times he feels that life won't let him be.
He feels tied down, unable to move. ~~~

He feels depressed and that his life is worthless. ~~~

Then something like a bright summer's day
or a beaming smile seems to make his life
worthwhile. ~~~

The Falling

Hypnotic trance,
rainbow minds dance
and even then
depression only blends,
never ends. ~~~

Blackened mind trance sadness full~~~

Will happiness ever call? ~~~

Of course not, don't be a fool;
your heart's a drained pool! ~~~

Hallucination, fascination, obsession,
aggression, but most of all depression.
With its beckoned call, my mind it mauls. ~~~

Your mind, is a swamp that crawls;
love an unreachable pearl.
If you could grasp it, would you
hurl it or clasp it? ~~~

Confusion sets in!
You lose control.
Help me,
Help us!
Death!

Depression rests?

Chapter 3:
Life

What is life?

Life is what you make of it.
To me, life is finding that one
special person, your soul mate;
that one person whom you want
to spend your whole life
and all eternity with.

That one person that sets your soul aflame,
who makes you want to leap out of bed at the
break of dawn just to see the sunrise?

Life is a strange thing.
I lie awake at night wondering
What is it all for this life?
What is the reason?
What is life trying to teach me?

Life has no meaning for me anymore
What is the reason I was put on this earth?
What is my purpose?
For all I seem to get is used,
abused, hurt, and pain.
If I'm lucky, life allows me a small
glimpse of happiness
for a while.

But then life as usual kicks me down
and everything I thought was good
just decays and I feel my life is meaningless
and worthless.

My mind runs wild and starts to throw doubts
and questions into the mixture.
Do I really have a reason for going on living?
I often ask myself.

Just when everything seems to be going great,
something comes along to destroy
my happy, contented little world.
If I was honest, would it really matter
to people around me if I wasn't around?
I wonder?

Is there a God?
I'm not sure because if there were,
why would he just sit there and allow all this
pain, hurt, and suffering to go on in the world?

I feel that the only true happiness
and freedom to be found is through death.

What is it all for this life?
Can somebody please explain?
For I just don't understand!

Broken

Why does life deal the cards?
It is as though somebody has decided to
cast the tarot and the cards for me are all the same.
Life is broken and there is no way to fix it.

My world is on permanent meltdown.
It is just as if I had found the self-destruct switch,
only to find that somebody had broken it permanently.

Just when I think that for once
in my pathetic ridiculous life
that something just might
for a change go right for me,
there's some nasty person
just waiting to kick me back
to reality.

It's as if there's a God looking down on me
and just as I start to feel as though this life might be
worth sticking around for,
He steps in and says "Ha-ha. I don't think so,
you're enjoying your life too much.

Let me see how I can smash things up for you,
I want to see how you deal with this broken,
smashed, battered, and disintegrating life.

You aren't allowed to be happy and contented because
that's not what I have planned for you.

I want you to go through as much pain, hurt, heartache,
bitterness, and disbelief in happiness as is possible.

So, every time that you feel safe, warm, and content
don't you forget that I am here waiting to smash
it to pieces.

Leaving your world and your life BROKEN.

The sparkle in you, little blue eyes,
will tell everyone you meet
just how special you really are~~~

So, hush little one, don't you cry,
for you are the apple of everyone's eye." ~~~

Falling Leaves

Gently do the seasons turn

in England's pleasant scene.

Softly do the autumn colours

tint the summer's green~~~

Amber, Copper, Chrome,

and Flame, Vermillion, and Gold.

The leaves in falling whisper

that the year is growing old. ~~~

Chapter 4:
Death

Reunion

Death is not the end, it is just a passing.

Like from one room to another.
Just as a butterfly emerges from a chrysalis,
so the human spirit frees itself from the earthly
body.

Just because you cannot see me,
don't shut me from your mind.
Think of me, pray for me, talk to me.
I'm as near to you as I ever was.
I can still stroke your cheek and ruffle your hair.

Nothing has changed between us.
I'm just a little way ahead, waiting,
and in a fraction of time, you will join me.
Everything will be as it always was, only infinitely
better.

We will always be together as one.

The Captive Dove

I'll not weep, because the summer's glory
must always end in gloom,
and follow out the happiest story~
It closes with a tomb! ~~~

And I am weary of the anguish
increasing winter bear.
Weary to watch the spirit languish
through years of dead despair. ~~~

So, if a tear, when thou art dying,
Should happily fall from me,
It is that my soul is sighing,
to go and rest with thee. ~~~

My Forever Pet

There's something missing from my home.
I feel it day and night.

I know it will take time and strength
before things feel quite right.

Though some might say "It's just a pet,"
I know I've lost a friend.

You've brought so much laughter to my home
and richness to my days.

A constant friend with joy or loss
with gentle loving ways.

Companion, Friend, and Confidante,
A Friend I won't forget.

You'll live forever in our Hearts,
Our Sweet Forever Pet.

Wings of Death

She built her wings out of all the death
that she had seen,
that had encased her within its clawed hands
as she journeyed along the path of pain
that time had carved.

Enduringly, she kept striving onwards
through all of life's trials, tribulations,
and obstacles that stood in her way.

She overcame it all and proved to herself,
if she could make it through all the worst
life had thrown in her pathway,
she would come out victorious,
and the warrior angel that she always
knew deep down she was.

Chapter 5: Mother

Mother

Take the M from Moonbeam,
lighting up the dark skies.
Take the O from Oasis,
in which heaven lies.

Then add T from Tenderness,
The H of Humility,
An E for Every kind of joy,
An R for Rare qualities.

Put them all together,
What do you think you've got?

It's MOTHER

and it's plain to see you're the best one of the lot!

A MOTHER is the heart of home~~~

Ring

Take a ring of solid gold,

with diamonds that sparkle and shine,

with emeralds and rubies all around,

as pure as rich red wine.

But even a ring so full of jewels,

like the one described above,

could not equal the joy of a mother,

and her strong and beautiful love.

She is all that is good and pure. ~~~

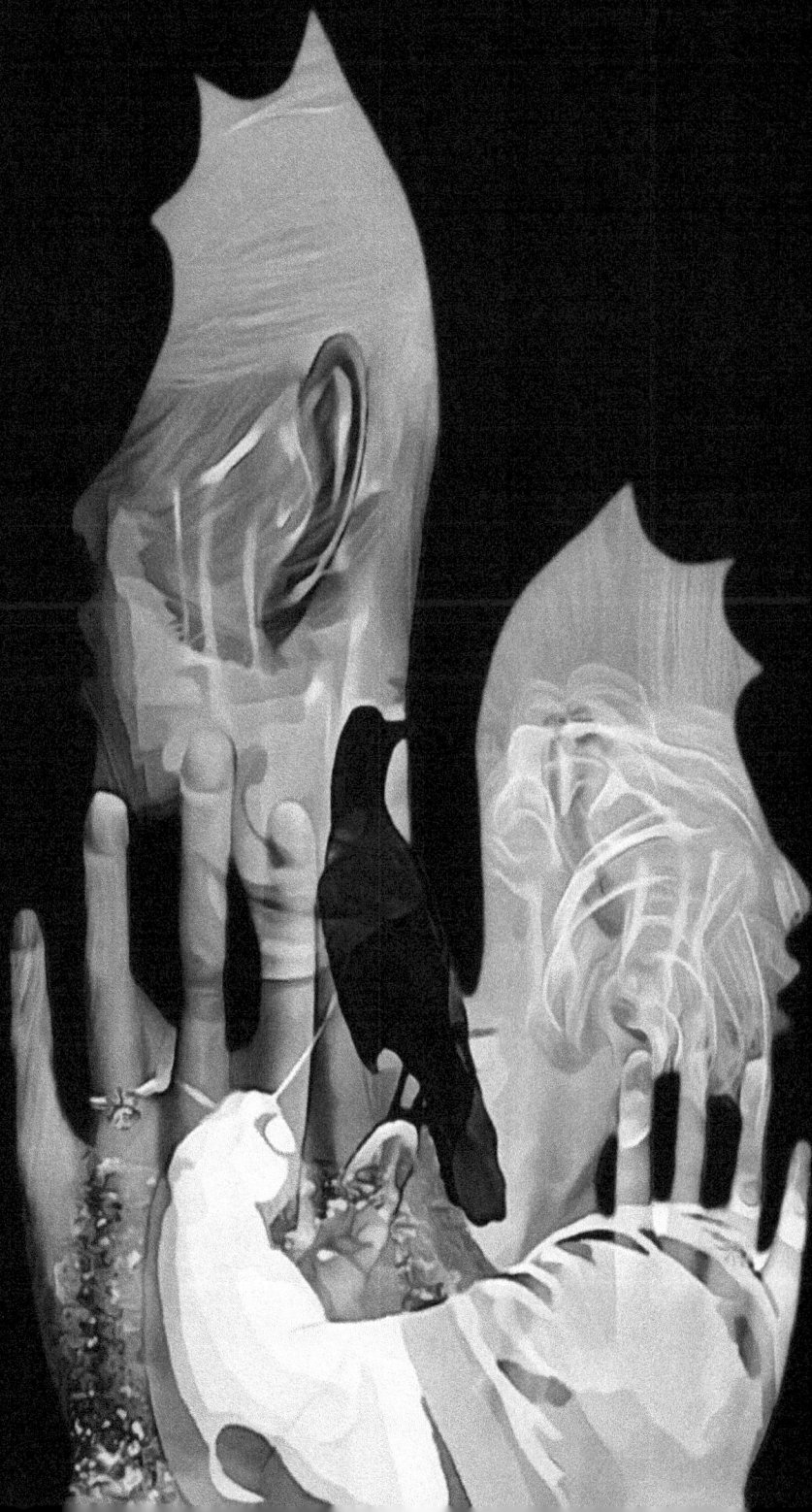

Things That Count

Life's really good, important things,

Are the simple things I've found,

A penny on the ground~~~

A true friend ~~~

A kindness found ~~~

A life that's free from care ~~~

And most of all a mother ~~~

Whose love is always there.

And the sweetest and dearest

Of Mothers is you ~~~

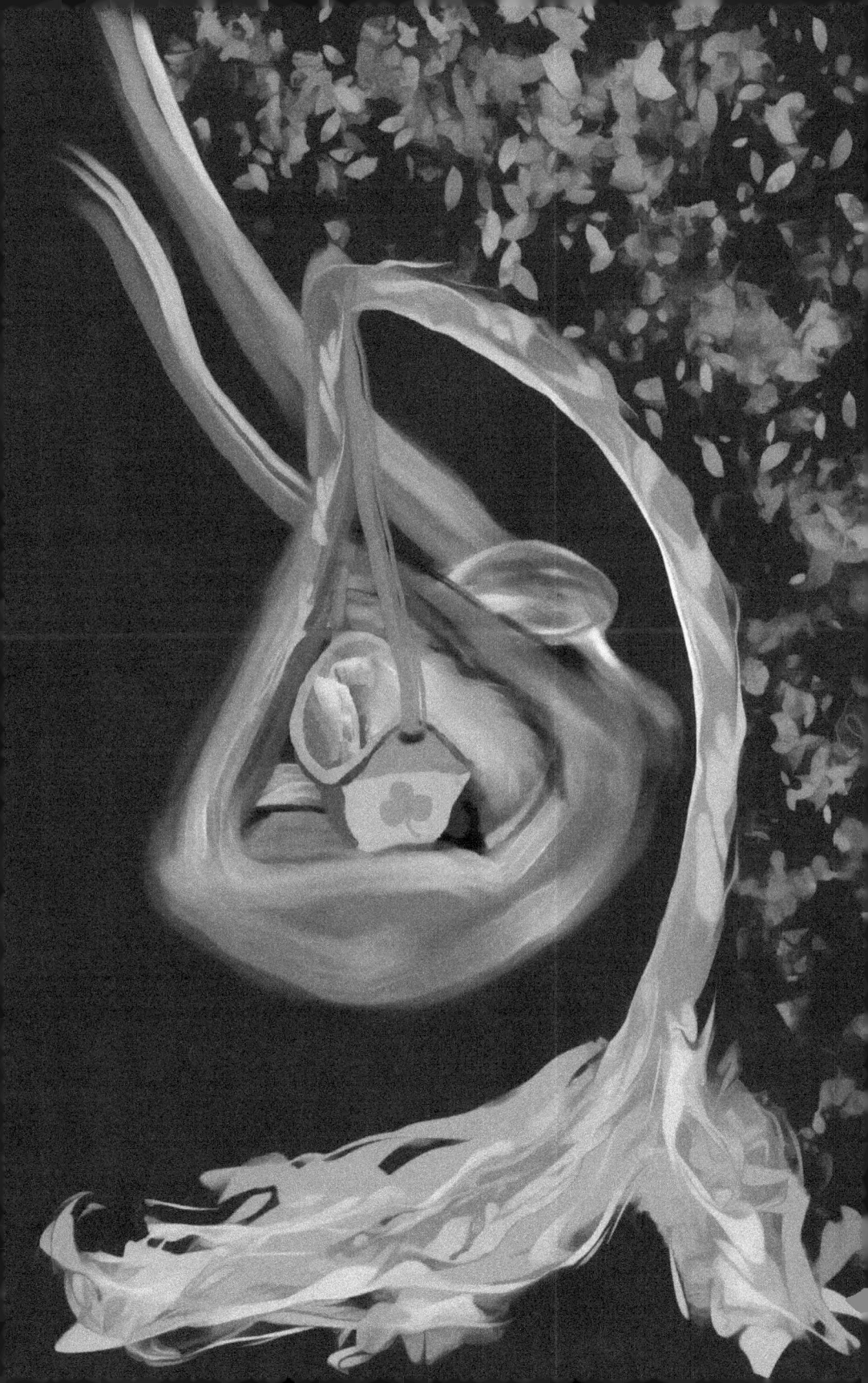

Chapter 6:
Friendship

Friendship

Friendship is a golden thread

That runs throughout the years. ~~~

And when we look back on the past,

that shining thread appears. ~~~

Eve

When God created woman,
he was working late on the sixth day. ~~~

An Angel came by and asked him,
"Why spend so much time on her Lord?"

The Lord replied, "Have you seen all
the specifications I have to meet to shape her?
She must function in all kinds of situations.
She must be able to embrace
several children at the same time,
have a hug that can heal anything
from a grazed knee to a broken heart.
She must do this with only two hands.
She cures herself when she is ill
and can work eighteen hours a day."

The Angel was overly impressed.
"Just two hands Lord......impossible!
And this is the standard model?"

The Angel then came closer
and touched the woman and said,
"But you have made her so soft, Lord."

"She is soft," said the Lord,
"But I have made her strong.
You can't imagine what she can overcome."

"Can she think?" asked the Angel.
The Lord answered, "Not only can she think,
she can reason and negotiate as well."

The Angel then touched her cheeks and said,
"Lord, it seems that your creation is leaking!
You have put too many burdens on her."

The Lord replied, "She is not leaking.... it is a tear."
The Lord corrected the Angel.

"What is it for?" the Angel asked.
The Lord replied, "Tears are her way of expressing
herself, her pride, her suffering, her loneliness, her
doubts, her grief, and her love."

This made a huge impression on the Angel.
"Lord, you are a genius, you have thought of everything.
A woman is indeed incredible. "

The Lord said, "Indeed she is."

She has strength that amazes a man.
She can handle any troubles
and can carry the heaviest of burdens.
She holds love, happiness, and opinions.
She smiles when she feels like screaming,
She sings when she feels like crying.
She cries when she is happy
and laughs when she's afraid.

She fights for what she believes in.
Her love is unconditional.

Her heart is broken when a next-of-kin or a friend dies,
but she finds the strength to carry-on with life.

The Angel then asked,
"So, she's a perfect being then?"

The Lord replied "No, she has just one flaw,
she often forgets just what she is worth."

A Way of Life

Go serenely amid life's noise and bustle.

Remember the peace that prevails in silence.

Be on good terms with all people. ~~~

Speak the truth quietly, but firmly.

Listen to others, even the dull and ignorant.

They too have something to say. ~~~

Avoid noise and aggressive people.

They are disturbing to human tranquility.

Comparing yourself to others may lead to envy.

There will always be greater or lesser persons than yourself. ~~~

Enjoy your successes and future prospects.

Be interested in your career, however humble.

Be cautious in your business affairs,

to avoid deceit.

But let this not blind you to people of great virtue. ~~~

Do not feign affection or be cynical about love.

They are a part of life's rich heritage.

Take kindly to the advance of years and be

charitable to the young citizens of tomorrow. ~~~

Be strong to fight adversity and misfortune.

Many fears are born of imaginings,

fatigue and loneliness.

You belong to the universe,

with all of nature's treasures.

You have the right to be a part of life. ~~~

Be at peace with God in whatever form you choose.

In the noisy battle and confusion of life, keep

peace with your soul. ~~~

Even with drudgery and broken aspirations, it

is an incredibly happy and beautiful world. ~~~

"Be Happy and Go in Peace."~~~

My Guardian Angel

The Guardian Angel is the being
to whom every soul is assigned.
They are there to help each-and-every one of us
prepare for the journey that awaits us here on earth.

They are there when the spark of divine light
enters the human form that the great spirit,
being of divinity sculpts with their hands
and life-giving breath.

In the moment when the spirit enters the sculptured
form, the Heavenly Host of Angels are standing by with
bated breath to learn if this perfect divine creation will
become their charge.

When they have their charge, it becomes their
responsibility as guardian Angels to teach, prepare and
ready their human spirit for their journey to the earthly
realm.

They send their charge down to earth with the
hidden knowledge planted like a small mustard
seed in the recesses of the mind.

Each spirit strives to find where and what its purpose
is on this plain, gaining knowledge along the path.
For our Guardian Angel softly whispers to our soul,

guiding us on our way.

Chapter 7: Feelings

Hope

Rapidly, merrily,
Life's sunny hours flit by.
Gratefully, cheerily,
Enjoy them as they fly!~~~

What though Death at times steps in,
And calls our Best away?
What though sorrow seems to win,

O'er hope, a heavy sway?
Yet, hope again shall spring,
unconquered though she fell,
still buoyant are her golden wings.
Still strong to bear us well. ~~~

Mournfully, fearfully,
the day of trial bares,
for gloriously, victoriously,
can courage quell despair! ~~~

Self-Interrogation

The evening passes fast away,
it's almost time to rest.
What thoughts have left the vanished day?
What feelings in thy breast? ~~~

The vanished day?
It leaves a sense of labors hardly done,
of little gained with vast expense,
a sense of grief alone! ~~~

Time stands before the door of Death,
upbraiding bitterly,
and conscience with exhausted breath
pours black reproach on me. ~~~

And though I've said that conscience lies
and time should fate condemn,
still sad repentance clouds my eyes
and makes me yield to them! ~~~

Then art' thou glad to seek repose?
Art' glad to leave the sea
and anchor all thy weary woes
in calm art? ~~~

Caught in a Love Triangle

Love shares such special feelings.
Just come into the moment when
you need me and I will do the same. ~~~

For somewhere in the silence of the moment,
I will hear you call my name.
For I am the deepest ocean,
I am higher than the highest mountain every day
if you're ever wondering where that love comes from,
you know that it is I.~~~

I am the air that fills your lungs your whole life through.
I am the sun that is warming you through.
I am there when you're watching the rain fall to the
ground. ~~~

You know that I'm there with you always,
as I know you are for me.
I am in you, as you are in me from now until eternity.
We will never part, as you are always
kept deep in my heart.
You live in me, as I do in you every day
and all through the night. ~~~

You seem to share all my thoughts
through the good times and the bad times.
You are always there just when I seem to need
you the most. ~~~

How strange it seems that we have become so
close to one another through all our times apart.
You will always live inside of me deep,
deep in my heart.

Where is the Trust?

Where is the trust?

I often ask myself, can I trust this man?

He tells me that we shouldn't fall.

That he fell and got severely burnt

and so to compensate for this,

he shuts himself off from any feelings

that could make him feel!

I ask you, where is the trust?

She once asked him if they would be honest

and truthful with one another; if he thought

it was possible.

He had told her that he had always told

her the truth and that he would never lie.

But at the first true blue time when she

needed him most, he had lied and let her down.

He had the best possible opportunity to pour

his heart out and his love into her,

but he found that he was unable and incapable

of telling her exactly what he was feeling within

the deepest recesses of his heart.

That there was something there as he looked

into the deep pools that were her eyes;

That he saw something that made him

wonder about this woman.

Would he, could he ever trust again?

Or was it all just a beautiful dream that lied to her?

Feelings

He is confused and unsure,

can't figure out what it is that he wants.

In his mind, the windows are clouded.

No matter how he tries, the light

just can't break through.

He doesn't know how to open up

and tell her what is in his heart.

So, to compensate for this, he cuts all strings

to his heart and feelings.

He puts himself on super freeze.

He shuts off and drinks to numb himself.

He can't feel.

He wants to die.

He just wants to be swallowed up in darkness.

He needs his space.

So, he pushes her away.

He doesn't realize that her feelings are slowly dying.

Their life goes on, but not the way it should.

It is almost as if this life they share

is half a life for both of them.

Soul searching for the answers that they just can't find.
Unspoken conversations that can
only happen face-to-face,
although face-to-face never is a conversation;
it only ends in arguments.

People get involved; chucking
their two cents in just makes things worse.
So, the two of them find themselves in a rut.
She pretends to be in control of the situation
where she is just fooling herself.

So, she takes off running as fast as she can
in the hopes that the feelings won't catch up with her.

But they always inevitability do and there's
nothing she can do about that.

In the season in which you are
meant to be all jolly and light,
they both find themselves overflowing
with darkness.

Neither one is able to cope
with the festivities of the season.
Both feeling and thinking the same thing,
but refusing to communicate.
Both putting on a show, pretending
everything is fine and dandy.

Time's a killer; the grim reaper of love.

Feelings so hard to traverse; one moment
you're ecstatic, next, deep tunnel of darkness.

Missing the tenderness, the love, the trust;
that sensual closeness that everyone craves,
cutting themselves up over what has been lost.

Trying so hard to find that magical feeling
of being in that warm wave of heat created
by two lovers in a love
where they find themselves soaring into
the stratosphere as they float away in ecstasy.

The Bitter Moon of Love

Wherever you may be,

I am still there for you.

You are not lost to me.

I shall still care for you.

I am not someone whom

you have once known,

taken away to leave you alone.

Tell me you love me deep in your heart.

Just speak my name.

We are not far apart.

Sus ojos para can pozos de fuego.

Chapter 8: Future

Why?

Why did you have to leave?

Why did you have to die?

Why did we not have the time?

What did I do so wrong?

Can someone please tell me?
Someone must have the answer.
Maybe someday we will be reunited.

Who knows?

It might be sooner than you think.
After all, what have I got here and now
to keep me tethered to this life and time I'm in?
Is this what they call life and living?

Well, if it is then if you don't mind,
I think I'll pass; thank you.

Why is it we don't get a choice

in what happens to us?

Şhạdẹş of Ḷịfẹ

What is it that draws us to certain people?

Is this God's sadistic sense of humour?

Or is it his plan to give us just a small
taste of what life could be?

Where, in reality, he doesn't really give a damn.

So, when things go wrong,
where do you think he is?

Well, if you don't know, I'll tell you.

His thought, I can't be bothered
so, you are on your own,
because I'm off on my sabbatical
and I'm not sure how long I'll be gone.
It could be nine months or nine years.
I haven't made up my mind.

So, I'll see you when I see you,
that's if you have managed to cope
on your own and manage to make it through.

If you are still about when I get back,

I might consider seeing you,

but I wouldn't count on it if I were you.

Tomorrow

There's always tomorrow,

so, look ahead

and take to the broader view.~~

There's always a new day on its way

with happier times for you. ~~

Out into the Sunshine

Out into the sunshine

may your steps be led

and good things await you

on the road ahead.

Fortune's fairest favors~~

Faithful friends and dear

on the winding roadway of another year. ~~

The Best is Yet to Be

The best is never over,

The best has never gone.

There is always something

lovely to keep you struggling on. ~~

There's compensation for every

cross you bare.

A secret consolation is hidden somewhere there. ~~

Ends are new beginnings as you

one day will see.

The best is never over. ~~

"The Best is Yet to Be!" ~~~

Give

Give your love to others,

don't spend it on yourself ~~~

Give your heart's good treasure,

don't hoard it on the shelf ~~~

Give a word of comfort.

Give a helping hand.

Try to understand. ~~~

Endless Wish

You don't understand

that sometimes I feel trapped.

That I can't break free from this life I lead. ~~~

I feel that I need some space

that's mine, and mine alone. ~~~

I can't explain what I am feeling.

It is at these times that I find that

all I wish and want to say doesn't

seem to make any sense. ~~~

It is then that all my words seem to desert me

and I am left alone, feeling

very dazed and confused. ~~~

Times when I want to break out and shout.

You treat me like a child at times and

make me feel stupid. ~~~

So, for once I'm going to scream.

I'm going to shout.

I'm going to be crazy.

I want to run free.

I want to be wild. ~~~

Sometimes I feel that I want to break free of this earthly body.

I want to fly far above the clouds in a large silver boat.

Do you think I can?

Do you think I'm mad? ~~~

I Feel!!

I get angry.

I get upset.

I get scared. ~~~

Do you understand?

Do you understand?

Do you care?

Do you even realize what I mean?

Do you know how I feel? ~~~

I look at you both and I feel covetous of you.

I know that I shouldn't, but I do:

I just can't help it. ~~~

You've both been so good to me.

You were there when nobody

else wanted to know me. ~~~

Sometimes I wish that I could step

out of my own shoes and into

somebody else's shoes for a change. ~~~

I sometimes wish I could have known you.

I want to know how you felt. ~~~

If you were happy?

If you were fun to be around?

If you got angry?

If you got upset?

If you got scared? ~~~

I wish I could take-a-look at a
snapshot of your life. ~~~

What did you think?

How did you feel?

Did you get dazed?

Did you get confused?

What made you laugh? ~~~

You found a way to escape.
I tried to escape, but I couldn't do it. ~~~

Maybe life has a wider and bigger plan for me! ~~~

What do you think?

Do you agree? ~~~

Am I a Ghost

Am I a ghost?
Sometimes I wonder;
do you think you can answer? ~~~

Am I a ghost?
It seems to me as though you
all look right through me...
Do you? ~~~

Am I a ghost?

I want to know!

You all make me feel so worthless,
as though I'm some dreadful chore
that nobody wants. ~~~

Do you understand? ~~~

Can you comprehend? ~~~

Do you realize what you're doing to me? ~~~

I don't think you do!

I think I understand what she went through!

I feel the same way!

You must realize that I am my own person! ~~~

That I feel,
That I get hurt ~~~

I don't know if you all realize what you do!
To tell the truth, I don't think you care ~~~

To me you all seem so superficial;
All caught up in your own self-importance ~~~

You are all in your own little world
and it doesn't seem to bother
or worry any of you
that you're possibly hurting anybody! ~~~

None of you care! ~~~

It is as though you are all on ice! ~~~

So, I ask you all once again ~~~

For you to answer me!!

Am I a Ghost?

Chapter 9: Dreams

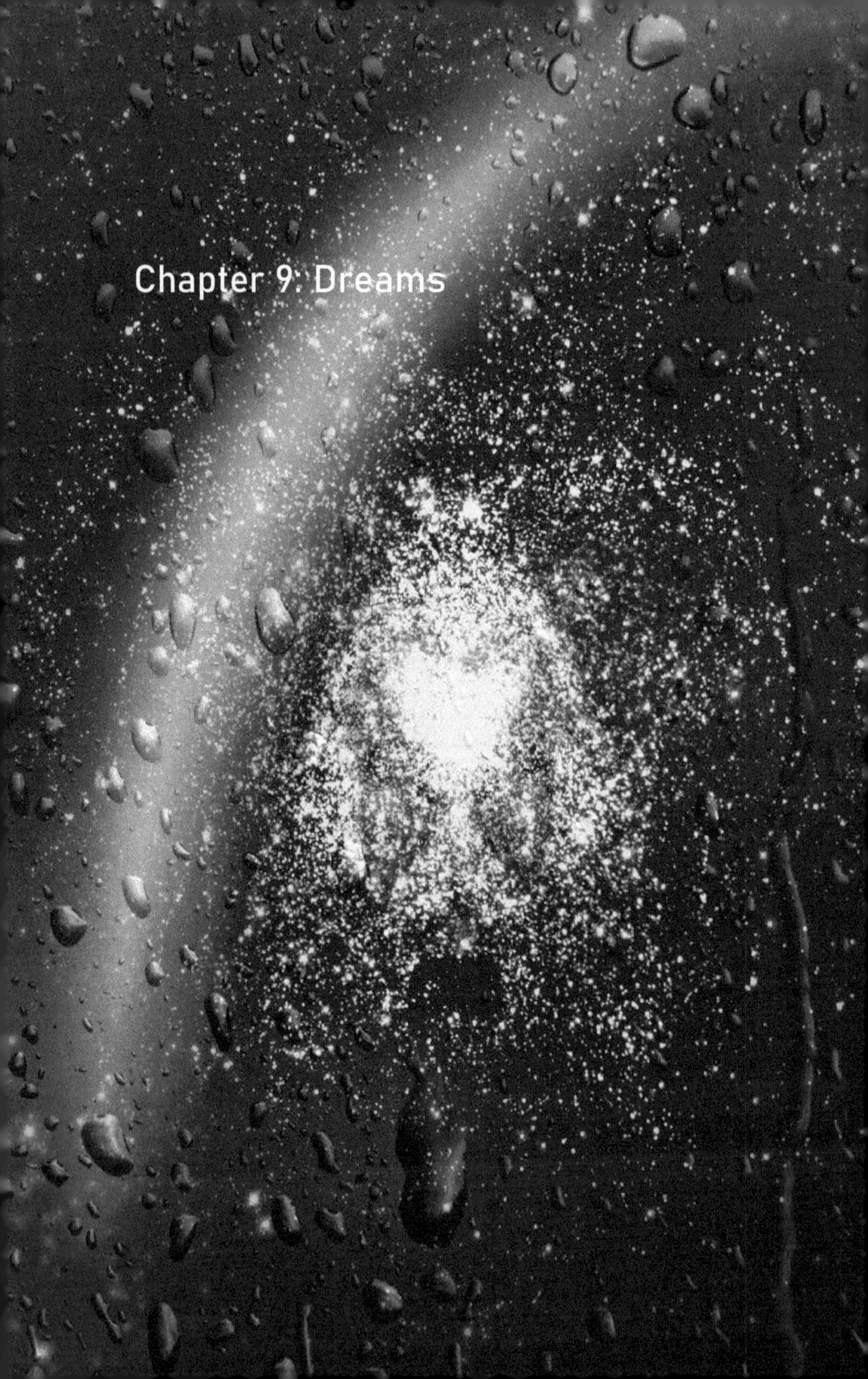

The Dream

Since man began to dream,

the idea of living on an island paradise

has fascinated him to the point of obsession. ~~

Visions of palm-fringed beaches,

clear blue seas and romance

filled evenings have seduced

him shamelessly. ~~

Sometimes to the extent

that real life begins to pale

and the only answer is to escape. ~~

Heart's Desire

In the working of a garden,

you discover much. ~~

As you watch the things you

plant respond to nature's touch. ~~

You are learning all the time

and never do you tire of

trying to create the garden

of your heart's desire. ~~

Chapter 10: Suicide

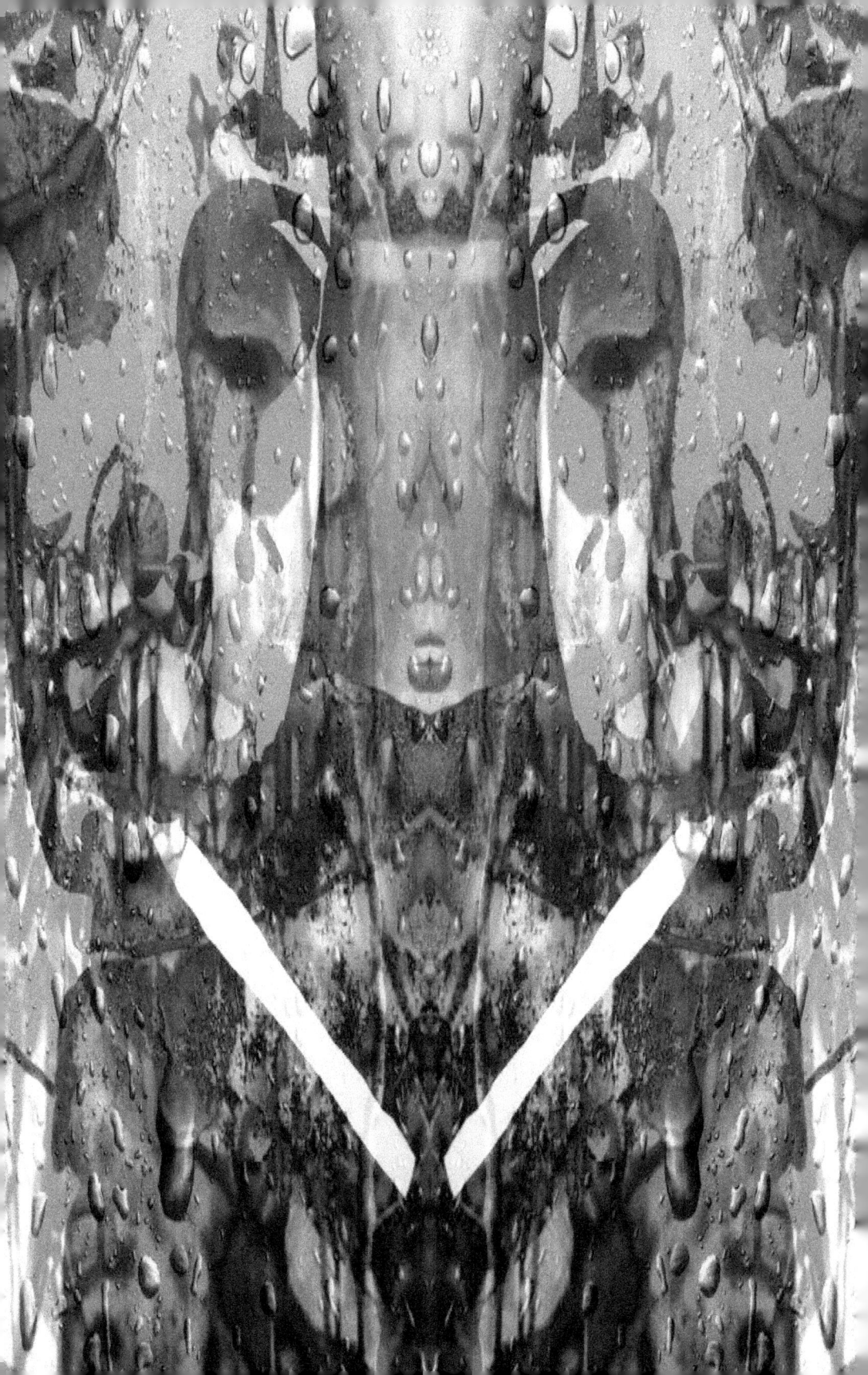

Disclaimer

Please be aware that the contents of this chapter address the thoughts, feelings, and experiences of the author during a dark time in their life. The author utilized the tool of writing to get the thoughts out of their head. The author considers therapy coupled with writing to be a powerful way to cope with suicidal ideation.

If you are at all feeling depressed, suicidal, or hopeless, please don't hesitate to seek professional medical advice and support in your area.

Canada: Talk Suicide Canada
  tel:1(833)456-4566
  sms:45645

USA: 988 Suicide and Crisis Lifeline
  988
  1(800) SUICIDE

United Kingdom: Samaritans UK & ROI
National
Hotline: +44 (0) 8457 90 90 90 (UK - local rate)
Hotline: +44 (0) 8457 90 91 92 (UK minicom)
Hotline: 1850 60 90 90 (ROI - local rate)
Hotline: 1850 60 90 91 (ROI minicom)

If your life is in danger, please call 911 (USA and Canada) or 999 (UK) right away or go to your nearest emergency department.

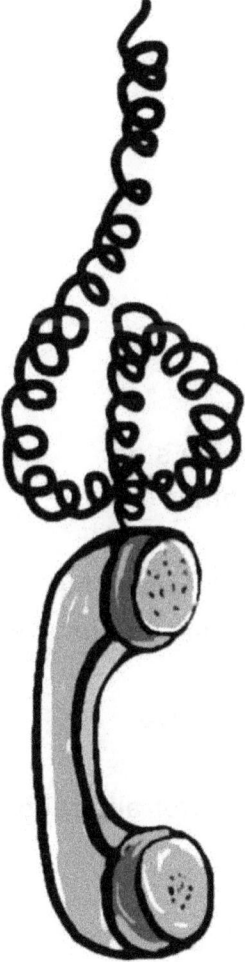

Remember that there is no shame in reaching out. There are people who care and if you give them a chance, they can help you in your time of need. So, do yourself a favor and reach out when you need help.

Nobody Knew

People used to tell her they understood:
that they knew just what she was going through
and that they knew exactly how she felt! ~~~

That they had been there
and come through the other side.
But nobody really knew.
Nobody could really understand
what she was feeling. ~~~

How at night she would wish upon a star
to be able to make it through another day. ~~~

Everyone had their own ideas about how she
should and ought to react to certain situations. ~~~

But she was rarely able to react or live
up to all their expectations. ~~~
So, she decided that it would be better all around
if she were to end it all. ~~~

But what she didn't understand that she
was always loved, and that she always would be! ~~~

Suicide

Blood oozing

out of my eyes,

...out of my mouth. ~~~

I think the best option is suicide,

but then how would I do it? ~~~

Have I the guts to slash my wrists?

Or perhaps jump in front of a train?

But both of the above would be messy! ~~~

I lay awake at night lately and think about

hanging myself.

How would I do it?

Where would I do it?

If anybody would find my motionless body

hanging there, limp? ~~~

I might just end up with a lot of broken

bones or paralyzed for life. ~~~

Maybe I should just take the cowards way out;

find some tablets and take as many as my body

can handle and take a few more for good measure. ~~~

I've tried that once before, but never really had the

courage to go through to the end and I've just stopped

at the second stage where your body is screaming that

it is being hurt. ~~~

Well, maybe it is time to take no notice of that sign

and just carry on until the end!! ~~~

After all, would it really matter?

Would anybody really care? ~~~

Sure, they would care and they

might even miss me for the first

couple of years if I'm lucky. ~~~

But then they would just go right on living

their lives. ~~~

I feel as though I'm drowning in a sea of

molasses and nobody wants to help me to get free!! ~~~

I lay here thinking about if I were in need of help,

Who would be there to help me? ~~~

I see quite a few people standing along

the shore of the molasses sea. ~~~

But all they seem to be doing is standing

there looking on. ~~~

I seem to be able to hold my head

above the molasses for a little while

and then I can't hold on any longer. ~~~

So, I finally find myself going under the sea

of molasses, then it goes black and it all ends.

Chapter 11: Ambition

The Seekers

Often, when you've scaled the peaks

Where stormy winds were shrieking,

You've found upon the lower slopes

The thing that you were seeking.

Dancer

She was stronger than they thought

and she danced her way through all

the carnage that others threw at her.

She drew on the strength that flowed

in her very life's blood; they could

cut and tear at her, but she still

continues to bloom through her

pain, her blood the invigorating

elixir that kept her going onward.

Give Us Back Our Lives

Give us back our lives.
Don't shatter our hopes and dreams,
for as you shall observe, things are
never what they seem. ~~~

You'll find out soon enough that
appearances can be deceptive
and that people try to fool you into
believing only what they want you to see,
because people are never quite
what they seem to be. ~~~

We communicate, but we never really speak,
for we refuse to truly hear
what our hearts already know.
We just fumble
and stumble our way through life. ~~~

Past generations didn't understand
and even now we continue to look
to the future to find the answers
to the unanswerable questions. ~~~

And so, to compensate for our own mistakes and
Misgivings, we start to build a utopia around us in
the hope that we might just disappear.
This allows us to pretend that everything is fine in
our broken and battered world. ~~~

But if we are honest with ourselves, we will see
that we are not really doing what we are in the
middle of doing at this precise moment in time.

But that we are just wandering around in a make-
believe world. ~~~

It is as if we are all in a deep, deep sleep;
that we seem to be sharing one dream
between us all. ~~~

There is only one difference between us;
we will all put different types of
situations into this dream state. ~~~

So, I ask you once again ~~~

Please, Give Us Back Our Lives. Don't shatter our hopes
and dreams. ~~~

Chapter 12: Solitary

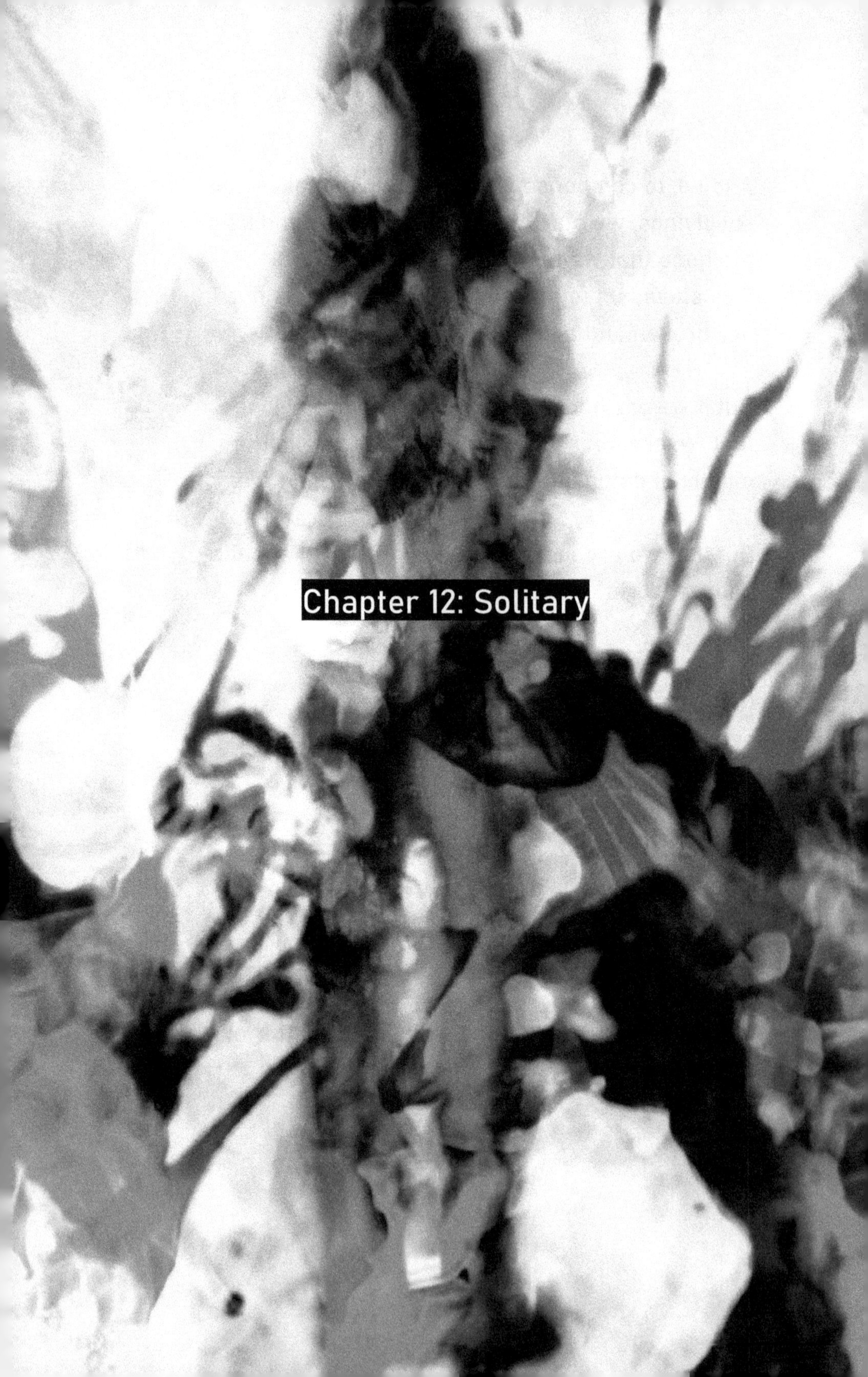

I Wish

Everybody guessed that the baby can't be blessed

'till she finally sees that she is like the rest.

Brightly beams our father's mercy from his lighthouse

ever more, but to us he gives the keeping of the lights
along the shore.

I wish I could write you a melody so plain that it would

save you, dear lady, from going insane.

That would ease you and cool you and cease the pain

of your useless and pointless knowledge. ~~~

Falling Through Space

Do you think that if you were falling through space,

you would go slow and see your world disappear?

Or would you find yourself going faster and faster?

If you were going faster and faster, do you think

that you would find yourself going so fast through

space that you would pass all the Angels that were

sent to protect you?

That you would find yourself falling so fast that

you couldn't stop yourself?

That you would burn up into a thousand tiny

pieces and be blown across space like the sands of
time? ~~~

Caged Dandelion

I'm imprisoned in childhood memories.

I wonder hopelessly,

who has the key?

Surrounded by people, completely alone. ~~

I'm tangled in a web of self-deceit.

Cut its threads

and uncage me.

A wild soul someday to be released,

Uncage me. ~~

Maybe someday I'll escape

and be forever free,

although you'll still be a part of me,

but until then I'll survive on dreams. ~~

I'm tangled in a web of self-deceit.

Cut its threads

and uncage me.

A wild soul someday to be released,

Uncage me. ~~

Sometimes I'm happy just to be

who I am,

As long as I fool myself

and believe the world is at peace,

but deep in my heart, I know,

Someone I'll never know is lying wounded

in a street to which I'll never go. ~~

I'm tangled in a web of self-deceit.

Cut its threads,

and uncage me.

A wild soul someday to be released,

Uncage me. ~~

I feel trapped and helpless,

Isn't there a way for you to set me free? ~~

I'm tangled in a web of self-deceit.

Cut its threads,

and uncage me.

A wild soul someday to be released,

Uncage me. ~~

I'm tangled in a web of self-deceit.

Cut its threads

and uncage me.

A wild soul someday to be released,

Uncage me. ~~

Give Me a Quiet Corner

Give me a quiet corner.

Give me a cottage far from

all the bustle of the towns.

Give me a garden I can tend

until the sun goes down.

Give me a quiet corner when

at night I close the door

and anyone can have the

world, I'll ask for nothing more.

Alone

Alone, completely isolated
from all that I have known.
Where did it all go?
It's as though it just vanished into thin air.
My life disappeared overnight.

Alone, empty like a discarded shell, no longer
of any use, a shadow of my former life.
No love here, no feeling left in my heart.

It's just as though I've been packed up into
a cardboard box and tossed into a cold, hard,
cruel world; I look around and find there is
nobody to whom I can turn to for guidance.

If only the hands of time could be turned back,
back to when you cared or gave a damn as to
what became of me.

But they can't,
so, I'm left once again abandoned
and alone,
to deal with whatever life decides
to throw my way in whatever way I can.

Things can never return to the way they were.
We can't talk to each other without
it turning into one almighty argument.

Alone, to cope my way, whatever that may be.

If love ever was there, it died a long time ago.
Now all you know of how to treat me is with
criticism, sarcasm and screaming insults my way.

Then you expect me to have respect for you and what
you say.

Well, I have news for you
and anybody who wants to listen to
anything I have to say.
Unfortunately, I don't have any respect
for you anymore.

For the simple fact is, that anger never lies.
People can't hide their true thoughts
and feelings in those moments of time.

We might not want to state our true
thoughts in those times, but all out emotions
take over any rational thought.

We say things to one another that we wouldn't
otherwise say and generally, what we speak
in those moments is the unadulterated truth
of what we think of others, that in a normal
scenario we wouldn't otherwise say out loud.

So now I know exactly what you think of me
and what you have always thought of me;
for that I will never be able to just forgive and forget.

Alone, completely alone!

Chapter 13: Memories

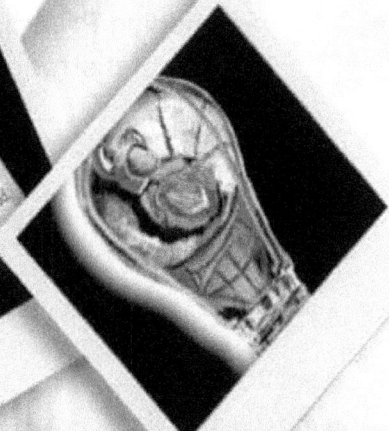

Memory

Brightly the sun of summer shone,
green field and waving woods upon,
and soft winds wandered by;
above, a sky of purest Blue;
around, bright flowers of love,
allure the gazers' eye. ~~~

But what were all these charms to me,
when one sweet breath of memory came
gently wafting by? ~~~

I close my eyes against the day
and called my willing soul away,
from earth, and air, and sky;
That I might simply fancy there. ~~~

One little flower - a promised Primrose fair,
just opening into sight as in the days of infancy;
an opening Primrose seems to me
a source of strange delight. ~~~

Sweet memory! Ever smile on me;
nature's chief beauties spring from thee.
Oh, still thy tribute brings,
still makes the Golden Crocus shine among
the flowers most divine.
The glory of the spring still
in the wallflowers' dwells;
and hover round the slight Bluebell,
my childhood's darling flowers. ~~~

Smile on the little Daisy still,
the Buttercups' bright goblet fill
with all thy former power. ~~~

Forever hang thy dreamy spell round the
Mountain Star and Heather Bell,
and don't pass away
from sparking frost
or weathered snow,
and whisper when the wild wind blow
or rippling waters play. ~~~

Never Again.

Use every hour of the day ~~~

Don't let the slip waste away....

Let something of value remain.

You'll never live this one again. ~~~

About the Author

I was born in Johannesburg, South Africa, in the 1970s. I lost my mother to depression at the age of 2 and was brought up by my father and his girlfriend until the age of 8 --- when I lost my father to cancer. After my father's passing, I was adopted by my aunt, and the family immigrated to America. I lived in America for 6 months, after which my aunt and uncle(s) made the decision to send me to a state children's home in England. I resided in state care until I was fostered by what I thought at the time was a loving family. Unfortunately, this turned out to be a very unpleasant time in my life. Later in my late 20s and mid-30s, I gave birth to three daughters and married the love of my life. Our marriage lasted for 10 years, until my husband became ill and passed away in 2014. Since then, I have met my current partner and live a quiet and happy life.

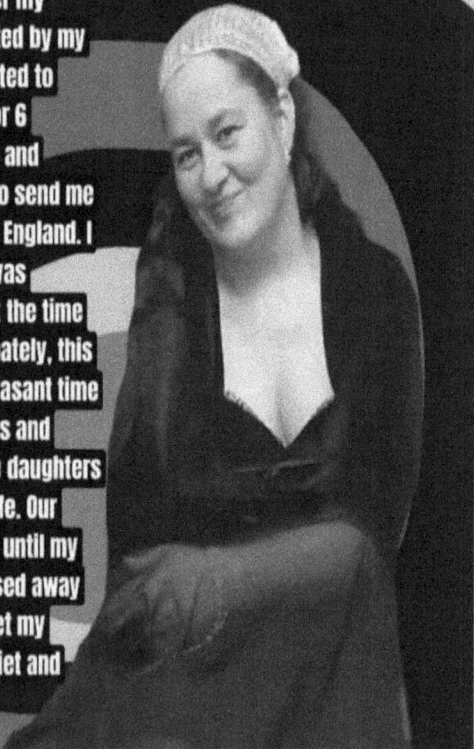

About the Illustrator

Marie Moldovan is a writer, artist, Canadian Forces veteran, jack-of-all-trades, and independent publisher at I Ain't Your Marionette. Shortly after he/r diagnosis with service-related PTSD and the passing of he/r husband in 2018, s/he began writing poetry to free he/r tormented mind. S/he is the author of 20 Years of Winter.

More from
I Ain't Your Marionette

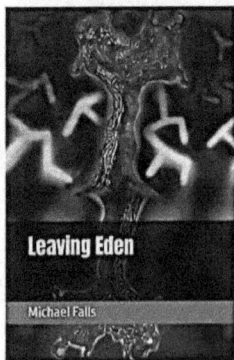